WOULD IT BE SO BAD TO SLIP FROM EXISTENCE?
WOULD IT BE SO BAD TO GIVE INTO THE DARKNESS?

Slipping From Existence

PERSEPHONE AUTUMN

SLIPPING FROM EXISTENCE

PERSEPHONE AUTUMN

BETWEEN WORDS PUBLISHING LLC

Slipping From Existence

Copyright © 2021 by Persephone Autumn

www.persephoneautumn.com

All rights reserved.

No part of this book may be reproduced in any form or by any electronic or mechanical means, including photocopying, information storage and retrieval systems, without written permission from the author except for the use of brief quotations in a book review.

This book is a work of fiction. Names, characters, establishments, organizations, and incidents are either products of the author's imagination or are used fictitiously to give a sense of authenticity. Any resemblance to actual events, places, or persons, living or dead, is entirely coincidental.

If you're reading this book and did not purchase it, or it was not purchased for your use only, then it was pirated illegally. Please purchase a copy of your own and respect the hard work of this author.

ISBN: 978-1-951477-36-3 (Ebook)

ISBN: 978-1-951477-37-0 (Paperback)

Editor: Ellie McLove | My Brother's Editor

Cover Design: Kat Savage | Kat Savage Designs

BOOKS BY PERSEPHONE AUTUMN

Poetry Collections

Ink Veins

Broken Metronome

Slipping From Existence

Bay Area Duet Series

Click Duet

Through the Lens

Time Exposure

Inked Duet

Fine Line

Love Buzz

Insomniac Duet

Restless Night

A Love So Bright

Artist Duet

Blank Canvas

Abstract Passion

Devotion Series

Distorted Devotion

Undying Devotion

Beloved Devotion

Darkest Devotion

Standalone Romance Novels

Depths Awakened

Sweet Tooth

Transcendental

Standalone Horror Novels

By Dawn (published under P. Autumn)

The past two years have been a struggle for many of us, me included.
Here's to finding a glimpse of light in the dark.

DO YOU SEE ME

Standing in the middle of the room
Do you see me?
Threading fingers through my hair
Do I exist?
In your face, screaming at the top of my lungs
Are my words coming across?
Fists flying
Feet kicking
Pleading
Begging
Crying for attention
I am here
Do you remember me?
Before I fade from existence
Do you see me?

FORGOTTEN

Your fingers on my skin
Lips on mine
It's been too long
Forgotten what it's like

The smell of your skin
Soothed my soul
But I've forgotten the scent
Hollow black hole

We slip into silence
Neither of us care
Conversations blank
As blank as my stare

An accessory

Arm candy
Brag-worthy material

Why?
Does it matter?

I am the forgotten

SOUL'S LAST BREATH

Beg
Borrow
Steal

Those shouldn't be
the themes of love

Touch
Taste
Collide

The pleas of the impassioned
woman on her knees

Eager
Willing

Wanton

The fire in my soul
slowly extinguishes

Fear
Sorrow
Existence

The truth of my life
The truth I must bear

JUST A DREAM

Love burns bright
White-hot heat
Sears my skin

A hiss on my lips
The bow of my back
Breasts peaked high

Your head between my thighs
Fingers slip inside

A moan
A growl
Impatience
Now

I wake with a startle
Hands between my legs
Pulse pounding against my ribcage

Solo act
again

Curl in on myself
Slam my eyes shut
Pleasure morphs to guilt

This is not love
Just a dream

JUST A GIRL

Wipe that look from your face
You don't get to smile
You don't get to be happy
You don't get to feel

Get off your ass
You have things to do
More important things
Things that make me happy

Know your place
You're just a girl
Another woman
And you have one job

Get in line

Work
Don't speak
You're just a girl

Make me happy
You're just a girl
A girl
Nothing more

Shut the fuck up
You're just a girl
A solemn creature
A voiceless servant

Do as you're told
Stay in line
Look the part
Smile when appropriate

You're just a girl
A meek soul
A replaceable shell
Just a girl

STRANGER

Damp walls
Cold heart
World around me
Falling apart

A slip
A crack
No longer caring
Refuse to fight back

Absence
Ache
Slowly morphs
Sudden hate

Loss

Fear
Black heart
Always here

Empty
Bare
A stranger
Without care

ROSE

Starts as a game
A little cat and mouse
The curve of your lips
How you trace your fingertips

A coy word here
A sly gesture there
Flirt
Smirk
Innuendo

Lips against mine
Hot
Wet
Energy

A world of lights
and sounds
The way the earth
pounds
An echo in the night
Glimpse pale moonlight

A beat so
rare
You've taken me
there

Until the petals drop
Slowly wilt black
Faint decomposition
No will to fight back

Light dims
Drifting out to sea
Unrecognizable life
Unrecognizable me

TUMULTUOUS CYCLE

Eb and
flow
Upside down
I go

Swing forward
Head high
Swing back
Familiar cry

Tumultuous
cycle
Keeps me in place

Tumultuous
cycle

Cannot replace

Tired
Shamed
No one else
to blame

Make it stop
Make it end
This tumultuous
cycle
In my head

ALONE

Too many days
Have I sat in this place
Alone
Tears pricking
the backs of my eyes

Too many nights
Have I laid in this bed
With you by my side
Alone
Tears spilling
down my cheeks

Wishing
Hoping
That maybe one day soon

I won't feel so
Alone

So empty
So unworthy

One day soon
I pray you will see me
Again
Will touch me
Again

Will make me feel less
Alone

INCAPABLE

Recently, I have felt
Incapable
Useless
An impostor in
my own skin

My drive
Desire
Spirit
Soaring on a dark cloud

Floating away
Vanishing

Taking all the pieces
which make me

Capable
Strong
Brave

Why did I do this?

Put myself here
In a position
Where I lack sufficiently
Where I fail easily
Where I fall gracefully

Why did I do this?

Punish myself
Say I was strong
Believe I was capable

Because all I feel
As I stare at blank pages

Incapable

STUTTERED

I tripped over myself
Hit the dirt and rocks
Skinned my knee
Scraped the flesh

And as I laid there
On my hands and knees
I questioned

The point in getting up
Of moving forward
Of trying again

One stutter after another
I fall to the earth
Get trampled by countless feet

Boot prints on my face
Pointed heels in my heart

And I lay there
Unwilling to lift myself up
Unable to reason why I should

Every step forward
is ten steps back
A crushed rib
A pierced heart

So I stay
Body blanketed in dust
And let the world
trample my broken
stuttered heart

SLIVER

I have given up
Stopped caring
what happens next
where things go from here
how this life matters

I have given up
Stopped asking
what matters
if I matter
if anything matters

What's the point?

Answers are
fruitless

another question
never an answer

And I'm so tired

Tired of making
every thought
every action
every decision

I have given up

But a small sliver
begs me
To hang in there
just a little longer

DARK MONSTER

The world has
gone to shit
A place
all too familiar

For once, it isn't just me
in the dark
For once, it isn't just me
rocking under
the shadow of misery

I should feel less
alone
sad
stigmatic

Somehow, though
The monster
in my veins
in my chemistry
in my makeup
craves more

The voice of doubt
speaks louder
taunts harder
torments harsher

It speaks of
pain
misery
despair
with a wicked smile on its face

Fight as I might
I will never be rid of
the darkness
the monster within

Because I am
the darkness
I am
the monster
And she is me

SAVE ME

The dawn of a new day
should bring
light
happiness
pleasure

But each morning
I peel the cotton from my body
and beg for
the night
the dark
sleep

The will to
try

continue
move forward
seems pointless

What once brought me
joy
Now mocks me
with a wicked gleam
and soul-crushing laughter

As once before
I have accepted this is
my life
my world
my existence

All I want
is one day

One day without
hurt
tears
darkness

And maybe, just maybe
That one day
will outshine every dark day

Maybe that one day
will save me

DARK FANTASY

For the first time in years
I thought of
the sharp sting of thin metal
as it pressed into skin
as it released pain
in a sea of red

For the first time in years
I remembered the
powdery taste of pills
too many pills
as they slid across my tongue
and fell down my throat

As always
These thoughts don't scare me

They are my past
A blip on the radar
that is my life

For the first time in years
I let these thoughts
swirl in my head
take up residence
own a piece of my present

Although I would never
let the razor slice my flesh anew
let the mound of pills roll down my throat
again
The fantasy of where it would take me
tempts
taunts
reminds

For I am the victim
and the assailant
Jekyll and Hyde
Two polar opposites
fighting to inhabit one soul
fighting for the limelight
fighting to take hold

Both will rise

As one cannot live
without the other
And
depending on the day
I may laugh alongside you
or weep for a better existence
A life without
teetering ideas and mental prisons

LOST DAYS

Lost are the days
When we would
talk
laugh
love
for more than one meal a day

Lost are the days
When I felt a sense of
importance
worth
significance
for my contribution to the world

Lost are the days
When I connected with

everyone
someone
anyone
for a single, measly minute

Lost are the days
When I
cared
smiled
hoped
for someone to do the same

FAIRYTALE

Once upon a time
A fairytale lived
in my mind

Not of
castles
royalty
or riches

A fairytale full of
light
love
and adventure

A fairytale of
gentle touches

rough kisses
and undeniable passion

But that fairytale
has shadowed
dimmed
faded to the background

That fairytale sits on
the edge
the precipice
the cliff
Waiting to see
which way the weight will
shift
tip
fall

Once upon a time
A fairytale lived
in my mind

If only I knew how
to make fairytales
come true

LIFELINE

Too many days, I am
a ghost
a specter
a forgotten soul

The lost girl, woman
screaming in her head
begging to feel
anything
other than the knife in her heart

The overlooked girl, woman
Not given another
thought
glance
word

as the world continues without her

The ignored girl, woman
Who tries to
matter
But can't find the
strength
courage
reason
when no one looks her direction as is

The girl, woman
Holding out a lifeline
begging
pleading
wailing
For someone to grab
the other end

SLIPPING FROM EXISTENCE

Who would notice
if I slipped from existence?
Who would notice
if I vanished without warning?

Days
Weeks
Months
may pass before someone asks,
"Where is she?"
"What happened?"

The reality of that truth
guts me
and pleases me
equally

For I have always been
the girl, woman
no one sees
no one thinks of
no one puts first

For I have always been
the girl, woman
too smart
too dark
too replaceable
too honest
too nagging
too... everything

Would it be so bad
to slip from existence?
Would it be so bad
to give in to the darkness?

The darkness
We are old friends
occasional acquaintances
buddies with a pinky promise
and inside jokes

The darkness never
judges me

holds expectations overhead
degrades me

In the dark
I feel it all
pain
sorrow
fear
hope
joy

In the dark
I let go

Give into the
soul-crushing
debilitating
need to please
everyone

Would it be so bad
if I slipped from existence?
Who would be the first
to know?

MORE BY PERSEPHONE AUTUMN

Ink Veins

Persephone Autumn's debut poetry collection, Ink Veins, explores topics of depression, love, and self-discovery with a raw, unfiltered voice.

Broken Metronome

When the music of the heart dies...

Broken Metronome is an angsty poetry collection full of heartache and the possibility of what may have been.

Transcendental

A musician in search of his muse and a woman grieving the loss of her husband. Two weeks at an exclusive retreat and their connection rivals all others. Until she leaves early without notice. But he refuses to give up until he finds her again.

Depths Awakened

A small town romance which captivates you from the start. Two broken souls have sworn off love. Vowed to never lose anyone else. But their undeniable attraction brings them together and refuses to let go.

The Click Duet

High school sweethearts torn apart. When fate gives them a second chance, one doesn't trust they won't be hurt again. Through the Lens (Click Duet #1) and Time Exposure (Click Duet #2) is an angsty, second chance, friends to lovers romance with all the feels.

The Inked Duet

A man with a broken heart and a woman scared to put herself out there. Love is never easy. Sometimes love rips you apart. Fine Line (Inked Duet #1) and Love Buzz (Inked Duet #2) is a second chance at love, single parent romance with a pinch of angst and dash of suspense.

THANK YOU

Thank you so much for reading **Slipping From Existence.** If you wouldn't mind taking a moment to leave a review on the retailer site where you made your purchase, Goodreads and/or BookBub, it would mean the world to me.

Reviews help other readers find and enjoy the book as well.

Much love,
    Persephone

CONNECT WITH PERSEPHONE

Connect with Persephone
www.persephoneautumn.com

Subscribe to Persephone's Newsletter
www.persephoneautumn.com/newsletter

Join Persephone's Reader Group
Persephone's Playground

Follow Persephone Online

- instagram.com/persephoneautumn
- facebook.com/persephoneautumnwrites
- tiktok.com/@persephoneautumn
- goodreads.com/persephoneautumn
- bookbub.com/authors/persephone-autumn
- amazon.com/author/persephoneautumn
- pinterest.com/persephoneautumn
- twitter.com/PersephoneAutum

ACKNOWLEDGMENTS

The past two years plus have been hard on us all. I simply want to say thank you and I love you to all the people that have stood beside me. On good and bad days, you were there.

Family and friends... I love you.

Ellie... thank you for the author Zoom meetings. Whether our small group chats are about book stuff or not, I loved having that small interaction with you and others. Hope to see your face again soon. Love you!

Kat... thank you for making my beautiful covers. And thanks for dealing with me occasionally annoying you. Love you!

Author peeps... when the world steals all the joy and we struggle with our creativity, I'm glad we have each other to virtually hug and rant and cry to. The past two years have been creatively challenging, but thank goodness we have each other. Love you all!

Readers and bloggers... you have no idea how much I appreciate each and every one of you. I look forward to the day when I can hug you in person. You made me smile during the darkest of days. For that, I cannot thank you enough. All the hugs!

ABOUT THE AUTHOR

Persephone Autumn lives in Florida with her wife, crazy dog, and two lover-boy cats. A proud mom with a cuckoo grandpup. An ethnic food enthusiast who has fun discovering ways to veganize her favorite non-vegan foods. If given the opportunity, she would intentionally get lost in nature.

For years, Persephone did some form of writing; mostly journaling or poetry. After pairing her poetry with images and posting them online, she began the journey of writing her first novel.

She mainly writes romance, but on occasion dips her toes in other works. Look for her poetry publications and a psychological horror under P. Autumn.

www.ingramcontent.com/pod-product-compliance
Lightning Source LLC
Chambersburg PA
CBHW030139100526
44592CB00011B/955